ᴅᴋ READERS

Level 3

Spacebusters: The Race to
  the Moon
Beastly Tales
Shark Attack!
Titanic
Invaders from Outer Space
Movie Magic
Plants Bite Back!
Time Traveller
Bermuda Triangle
Tiger Tales
Aladdin
Heidi
Zeppelin: The Age of the
  Airship

Spies
Terror on the Amazon
Disasters at Sea
The Story of Anne Frank
Extreme Sports
Spiders' Secrets
The Big Dinosaur Dig
The Story of Chocolate
School Days Around the World
LEGO: Mission to the Arctic
Star Wars: Star Pilot
The X-Men School
Fantastic Four: The World's Greatest
  Superteam

Level 4

Days of the Knights
Volcanoes and Other Natural Disasters
Secrets of the Mummies
Pirates! Raiders of the High Seas
Horse Heroes
Trojan Horse
Micro Monsters
Going for Gold!
Extreme Machines
Flying Ace: The Story of Amelia
  Earhart
Robin Hood
Black Beauty
Free at Last! The Story of
  Martin Luther King, Jr.
Joan of Arc
Welcome to The Globe! The
  Story of Shakespeare's Theatre
Spooky Spinechillers
Antarctic Adventure
Space Station: Accident on Mir
Atlantis: The Lost City?
Dinosaur Detectives
Danger on the Mountain: Scaling the
  World's Highest Peaks
Crime Busters
The Story of Muhammad Ali
First Flight: The Story of the
  Wright Brothers
D-day Landings: The Story of
  the Allied Invasion
Solo Sailing
LEGO: Race for Survival

WCW: Going for Goldberg
WCW: Feel the Sting
WCW: Fit for the Title
WCW: Finishing Moves
JLA: Batman's Guide to Crime
  and Detection
JLA: Superman's Guide to the Universe
JLA: Aquaman's Guide to the Oceans
JLA: Wonder Woman's Book of Myths
JLA: The Flash's Book of Speed
JLA: Green Lantern's Book of
  Inventions
The Story of the X-Men: How it all Began
Creating the X-Men: How Comic Books
  Come to Life
Spider-Man's Amazing Powers
The Story of Spider-Man
The Incredible Hulk's Book of Strength
The Story of the Incredible Hulk
Transformers Armada: The Awakening
Transformers Armada: The Quest
Transformers Armada: The Unicron
  Battles
Transformers Armada: The Uprising
Transformers Energon: Megatron Returns
Transformers Energon: Terrorcon Attack
Star Wars: Galactic Crisis
Graphic Readers: Curse of the Crocodile
  God
Graphic Readers: Instruments of Death
Graphic Readers: The Price of Victory
Graphic Readers: The Terror Trail
Fantastic Four: Evil Adversaries

A Note to Parents and Teachers

DK READERS is a compelling programme for beginning readers, designed in conjunction with literacy experts, including Maureen Fernandes, B.Ed (Hons). Maureen has spent many years teaching literacy, both in the classroom and as a consultant in schools.

Beautiful illustrations and superb full-colour photographs combine with engaging, easy-to-read stories to offer a fresh approach to each subject in the series.

Each DK READER is guaranteed to capture a child's interest while developing his or her reading skills, general knowledge and love of reading.

The five levels of DK READERS are aimed at different reading abilities, enabling you to choose the books that are exactly right for your child:

Pre-level 1: Learning to read

Level 1: Beginning to read

Level 2: Beginning to read alone

Level 3: Reading alone

Level 4: Proficient readers

The "normal" age at which a child begins to read can be anywhere from three to eight years old. Adult participation through the lower levels is very helpful for providing encouragement, discussing storylines and sounding out unfamiliar words.

No matter which level you select, you can be sure that you are helping your child learn to read, then read to learn!

LONDON, NEW YORK, MUNICH,
MELBOURNE, and DELHI

Designer Lisa Crowe
Project Editor Amy Junor
Senior Art Editor Lisa Lanzarini
Publishing Manager Simon Beecroft
Category Publisher Alex Allan
Production Editor Sean Daly
Print Production Nick Seston

Reading Consultant
Linda Gambrell

First published in the United States in 2008
by DK Publishing
375 Hudson Street
New York, New York 10014

08 09 10 11 10 9 8 7 6 5 4 3 2 1
DD398—11/07

DK books are available at special discounts when purchased in
bulk for sales promotions, premiums, fund-raising, or educational use.
For details, contact:
DK Publishing Special Markets, 375 Hudson Street, New York, New
York 10014
SpecialSales@dk.com

ISBN 978-0-7566-3828-3 (Hardback)
ISBN 978-0-7566-3829-0 (Paperback)

High resolution workflow by Media Development and Printing Ltd, UK.
Printed and bound by L-Rex, China.

Discover more at
www.dk.com

DK Readers

PROFICIENT
4
READERS

Skate!

Written by Amy Junor

DK

Stance
To balance
properly on a
skateboard, ride
looking straight
ahead and bend
your knees.

Clothes
Wide shoes with
good grip and
comfortable
clothes are best
for skating and
doing tricks.

"Mom!" calls Gus. "Where's my
black Tony Hawk t-shirt?"

"I don't know honey. In one of the
boxes, I expect."

Gus looks around their new house
at the stacks of cardboard boxes.

A couple of the boxes are labeled 'Bathroom' in large, black letters. Some are labeled 'Dining Room', and a lot have 'Kitchen' written on them. He finds a box labelled 'Gus' and rips it open, spilling the contents all over the floor.

"Careful you don't make a mess!" his mom yells out.

"Yep," shrugs Gus, pulling his black t-shirt from the pile and ducking out the front door before his mum discovers his stuff all over the floor.

It's always hard moving house, moving schools, making new friends. But the one thing Gus always has is his skateboard.

Skateparks are where Gus has always made new friends. A couple of great ollies and a few good kickflips and everyone wants to be friends with him.

But here, somehow, it's different.

Art
Some decks have amazing artwork underneath, but can still be decorated with stickers or drawings.

Safety
When skating, always wear knee-pads, elbow-pads, and a helmet and learn how to fall properly.

5

Grab

Holding the board with your hands when you are in mid-air during a brilliant trick is called a grab.

Daryl is the best skater at the local skatepark and plans that he always will be. He doesn't like Gus because he is a really good skater.

Gus sees two other skaters from his new school. Taylor and Fran recognize Gus too, but they don't say hello because they are Daryl's friends.

Daryl pulls off a stylish jump, glares at Gus and laughs with Fran and Taylor. Gus tries a kickflip, but stumbles when he lands and his board rolls away. Daryl laughs at him in front of everyone.

"Good luck in the competition. You'll need it!" Daryl yells. Gus's face turns red, but he gets ready to kickflip again. As he pushes off, he thinks about what Daryl said. There's a competition to get on the local team which means sponsorship and the first step to turning pro. That's the main reason Gus entered, but it was also a way to try and fit in here.

Deck
The wooden part of a board is called the deck. The front of the board is called the nose and the back of the board is called the tail.

Branding
There are loads of different skate brands. Shop around until you find one that you like.

Street skating
Skating street means skating on curbs, steps, and pavements found in the urban landscape.

Vert skating
Skating on half-pipes, ramps, and rails that have been made especially for skating is called vert skating.

Instead, because Daryl has entered too, he thinks Gus is trying to take over. And the worst thing? The competition is tomorrow.

Gus ollies into the air, flips his board, and concentrates on his landing. It's perfect. He smiles, pleased with himself, but can't find the courage to say anything back to Daryl. Daryl skates off.

Taylor and Fran stick around. Taylor is really good at lots of tricks, but always lands badly from jumps. Taylor tries a nollie, but lands with his back foot in the middle of the board.

"Hey Taylor," says Gus. "You'll snap your deck if you don't land your foot over the back trucks."

Taylor looks over his shoulder to see if Daryl is still in hearing distance.

"Yeah, because your kickflip landing was so great," says Taylor.

"It'll snap," Gus mutters, skating off.

Vert ramp
Pro-legend Tony Hawk performs a trick on a vert ramp, which is a half-pipe with vertical sides.

Grip tape
A sandpaper-like tape called grip tape is stuck across the top of the deck so that the board doesn't slip during amazing tricks.

Half-pipe
A half-pipe is like a cylindrical pipe cut in half and made of concrete.

Different sizes
Half-pipes can be indoors or outdoors and come in different sizes and steepness.

Dropping in on a half-pipe always makes Gus feel better, no matter what is going on. The adrenaline rush from first dropping in is the best feeling he's ever known.

Gus sets up with the tail of his deck on the rim of the ramp and feels his balance. He breathes in slowly, then moves his weight forward and drops in.

As he gathers speed, Gus feels nervous. He's not sure he's ready for the competition tomorrow. What if he gets on the team and Daryl doesn't? Will that make life here harder? What if Daryl gets in and he doesn't? How will he face the other skateboarders then? Maybe he should go to another skatepark!

This is the first time in Gus's life that the half-pipe hasn't cleared his head. He lands on the rim, grabs his board and walks over to the indoor half-pipe by himself.

Gus leans against the wall inside. He can see Taylor skating in the indoor half-pipe.

Taylor looks annoyed as he pumps to get more speed. Gus watches Taylor as he bends his knees each time he gets to the bottom of the pipe and then straightens them as he rides up the sides. Taylor gets faster and faster, but doesn't attempt any tricks. Gus is dying to show him some tricks he could do, but he doesn't dare.

The one thing that Gus has been trying to nail for ages is his axle stall on the top of the half-pipe.

Watching Taylor in the half-pipe now, he really wants to show him how to do it and get in some practice. Taylor sees Gus watching him and goes outside again.

Gus drops in, pumps to pick up speed, then pulls off a nearly perfect axle stall on the rim of the half-pipe.

Crouch
To go faster, lean forward, crouching, at the bottom of the pipe. Straighten your legs as you ride up the other side.

Fakie
When you reach the top of the half-pipe, switch to fakie stance, riding backwards, without moving your feet.

Obstacles

Doing tricks on a low rail in a skatepark is good practice for similar obstacles in the urban landscape.

Taylor is practicing his boardslides on a low rail. He skates toward the rail at an angle, ollies up, and turns in the air. Taylor lands straddling the rail with the middle of the board and grinds down it. He twists off the end and lands a bit awkwardly, but still, he does it! Gus is impressed.

"Nice one," says Gus.

Taylor ignores him and rides off.

Taylor is pretty confident now that he's landed his boardslide like a pro with everyone watching!

He pulls off a 50-50 grind that he's been practicing for weeks.

Taylor ollies up onto a rail and lands his trucks on the rail this time instead of the middle of the board like a boardslide and grinds down the rail.

Taylor does really well, but Gus is too nervous to tell him it was good in case he is ignored again.

Balance
Balance is crucial for this trick because the middle of the board must travel along the rail without falling off!

Height
It's important to lift your front foot really high so that the board gets enough height to land on the rail.

Now that Taylor is on a roll, Daryl and Fran take a break to come over and watch him. Leaning against the wall, they stare at Gus as he grabs his board and joins them. Taylor starts to show off his nollies. He lands with his back foot in the middle of the board everytime, and everytime Gus flinches. But he doesn't say anything. Gus looks over at Daryl to see if he's noticing. Daryl is smirking. It looks like he knows but doesn't want to help Taylor at all.

Landing
It's important to land with your feet over the trucks so that they absorb the impact of your landing.

Fresh tips
Watching other skaters is a great way to pick up tips that can improve your own tricks.

Taylor nollies one more time. As Gus watches, it seems like everything is happening in slow motion.

Taylor pops the tail of his board and flies into the air. He pulls his back foot up so that he can get more height—so far this trick is looking perfect.

But then the board comes down. Taylor's foot doesn't move back to land above the board's back trucks.

Taylor lands. His foot is in the middle of the board. SNAP!

His foot goes straight through the board and the two halves of the deck fly out in opposite directions. Pieces of wood are scattered into the air.

Gus feels awful, but Daryl just laughs. Taylor's eyes well up with tears. He grabs the two remaining halves of his board and walks away.

Grip tape
The tape across the top of the deck is called grip tape. It helps your feet to grip the board.

Crouch
Crouching down really low will help get maximum height when you pop the nose.

"Oh that was classic!" laughs Daryl as he turns and pushes off on his board.

To show up Taylor's disasterous nollie, Daryl pulls a perfect nollie 180. He nollies into the air, twists 180 degrees, lands stylishly, and skates away.

Gus looks over to Fran and shrugs. He really doesn't know what to say. Gus can't believe how bad Daryl is acting and he can see by the look on Fran's face that she agrees with him.

"Um..." Gus really wants to say something. He tries to think of the right thing to say.

"Do you think Taylor will be ok?" he asks finally.

Fran tugs at her hair.

"I guess. I mean, I hope so," she says quietly, looking at the ground.

They both stand there trying to think of the next thing to say.

Fran slowly starts to tic-tac while she thinks. It always helps her to think properly when she is walking or skating or just moving somehow.

"You ride goofy," says Gus.

"Yep, I'm left footed," Fran replies and pauses awkwardly. "You know, I asked Daryl how I could make my ollies better, but he wouldn't really help. He just wanted to show off, I guess. He never really explained how to do anything."

"Maybe I can help," offers Gus. "That is, if you want me to. I won't if you don't want me to."

"No, that would be great!" answers Fran, smiling at him. "Is it really different though, you know, because I ride goofy?"

"Well, not really. It's just that you do everything the other way around. I'll show you how I do it and then try to do it goofy back-to-front. But I'll explain it as well as I can."

Goofy
Most people skate with their right foot forward. Fran feels natural with her left foot forward, but she still tries to practice with her right.

Hair safety
If you have long hair, keep it out of the way by tying it back when you're skating, or wear a cap.

23

Landing

To complete a perfect landing, aim to land on all four wheels at the same time and don't forget to crouch down!

Gus shows Fran a perfect ollie. Many skate tricks are based on ollies, so it's important to get them right. Being able to do them well makes other, harder tricks, easier.

"When you ollie," says Gus, "first you have to snap the nose down really hard. Don't be scared of doing it really hard or you won't get enough height."

Fran practices snapping the nose of her board a few times. "Yep, I get it. I don't think I was doing it hard enough before."

"Ok, so when you're in the air, straight away make sure you drag your front foot right up to the nose and your back foot up in the air so that the board can come up to meet your foot. You've gotta kind of crouch up in the air."

Daryl is watching them and glaring over. Gus feels a bit nervous, but he's really enjoying finally having a friend here!

Popping
To ollie, pop the board's nose by pushing the tail down hard onto the ground and taking the weight off the front foot.

Technique
Drag your front foot up to the nose as soon as you lift your back foot so the board can fly into the air.

Frontside
When a trick is performed with your front facing the step or obstacle, like here, it is called a frontside trick.

Backside
If you're facing away from the obstacle or step, this is called doing a trick backside.

Gus is having so much fun showing Fran how to do an ollie. She's getting it too! She can pop the nose hard now and gets a decent amount of height. Once she remembers to drag her feet up, and land properly, she'll be really good. Daryl is still keeping an eye on them.

"Fran," asks Gus, "maybe I can show you a frontside ollie?"

"Sure!" she answers, popping the nose of her board again. It's so much fun now that she knows how to do it properly.

Gus ollies into the air facing the other way. He gets a lot of height and rides away with style. For the first time today, he feels really good. And the selection for the team suddenly doesn't seem as all-important as it did a short while ago!

"You're a really, really good skater, Gus. You'll be fine tomorrow in the competition," says Fran, just as Daryl happens to skate over and hear her.

Grinding
To feel the grind, lean back a little at the same time as both trucks land on the edge of the obstacle.

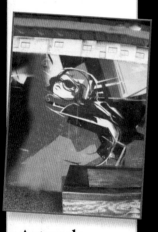

Artwork
Many skaters are good artists too! Most skateparks have incredible street art and colorful murals.

"Oh yeah, you're really great," mimics Daryl. "You would get on the team for sure. Except that I'm going to beat you."

"Don't be so sure," mumbles Fran.

"What do you know about skating?" Daryl snarls at her. "So," he turns back to Gus. "What's your best trick then, new kid?"

"I don't know. I can do loads of things." Gus now feels a bit nervous with Daryl glaring down at him.

"Well, can you do this?" Daryl skates up to a rail, ollies up, and pulls a wicked nosegrind down it.

"Of course he can!" says Fran.

"Of course he can!" mimics Daryl. "Go on then, new kid," he dares Gus. "Get up there."

"I would...but it's a bit too easy," braves Gus.

"Oh come on, impress me," Daryl says, rolling his eyes and leaning on his board.

Ollie
Even a heelflip starts with an ollie, which is why it's really important to master ollies before you move on to any other tricks.

Gus pushes off and skates a short distance away from them, thinking of the best trick to do. It has to be one that he can definitely pull off without embarrassing himself.

He's always been really good at heelflips and can get really high in the air.

Gus turns back to Fran and Daryl and skates towards them, determined to pull the best heelflip of his life. He gathers speed, pops the nose, and flies high into the air.

Within seconds, Gus flips his board completely around and lands perfectly in a crouch. He rolls to a stop just in front of Fran and Daryl.

Daryl is silent. Fran is smiling.

"Well, that is pretty impressive," says Fran.

Daryl can't think of anything to say. He is really annoyed.

"Well I guess I'll be seeing you tomorrow then, new kid," he grumbles. "Good luck."

Arms
Using your arms to help you balance is the best way to make sure that you land well.

Flip
To do the flip in a kickflip, the heel of the foot catches the edge of the board and flips it over.

Daryl grabs his board, ollies up onto a stair rail, skates down it, and out of the skatepark.

"That was really ace," smiles Fran.

"Let's go see if Taylor's ok," says Gus.

They find him slumped in a corner of the indoor part of the park, with the pieces of his board around him. His eyes are red and puffy.

"Hey," says Gus.

"Go away," says Taylor.

"It's ok," Fran tells him. "Gus showed up Daryl and he's thrown a tantrum and left! It was great! I wish you'd been there."

"Really?" asks Taylor.

"Well, I don't know that I showed him up exactly, but he's gone," says Gus.

"Of course you did. Stop being so modest. Now you really have to beat him tomorrow. Let's get some more practice in. We're not as good as you but we'll help you if we can."

"Thanks guys," smiles Gus.

Practice
Mastering tricks properly on low objects like this rail makes it easier to skate on more difficult railings.

Rail slide
Skating down high and long railings should only be attempted by very experienced skateboarders.

"Hey Taylor," says Gus. "Do you want to come to the skateshop later? I've got a gift certificate for my birthday, maybe we could use it to get you a new deck."

"I couldn't take your gift certificate, Gus. It's for your birthday," Taylor replies.

"Honestly. I've already got two boards. I just need some new wheels. You can have the rest."

"Um, thanks Gus," shrugs Taylor. "You know, you're alright."

Gus feels good for the first time today. And now he is going to get some practice in and Daryl isn't!

"Taylor, your boardslide before was really good. Show me how you did it," says Gus. He might be a great skater, but Gus knows that you can learn a lot from other skaters. You could pick up any sort of little trick that you hadn't thought about! Taylor shows them his boardslide again, and then they watch Gus practice down the rail.

"Cool," says Gus, "let's go to the shop."

Anywhere
Any raised surface or step can be used to jump off and do a trick.

Share
Skate parks aren't just for skaters. Watch out for others using the park and keep out of their way.

"Hang on," says Fran. "Taylor missed your heelflip. It was pretty good. Why don't you show Taylor before we go to the shop."

"Well, I don't really like showing off..." Gus mumbles.

"C'mon. I want to see how a pro does it!" smiles Taylor.

Gus pushes off, ollies up, and heelflips again. Both of his new friends are impressed. They laugh and clap. Gus smiles.

"Well maybe I can do a kickflip too?" asks Gus.

"Brilliant!" says Fran.

He gets up some speed, ollies into the air and kickflips a full 360.

Fran whistles and claps. Everyone at the skatepark looks over. Gus does another kickflip.

Now a small crowd is watching. Gus starts to feel a bit embarrassed.

"C'mon, lets go to the skate shop," he says.

Expert advice

People who work in skate shops are often skaters too, so they will give you great advice about what you need.

Displays

Decks are displayed upside down to show their amazing designs underneath.

The beaded curtain on the door of the skateshop rattles and shimmers as they walk through it. Gus, Taylor, and Fran head straight for the brightly colored decks at the back of the shop. There are so many to choose from. Taylor fiddles with the old trucks and wheels in his hands.

"Maybe you should get one with a skull on it," says Fran.

"Maybe you should get a blank one so you can paint it or put stickers on it," suggests Gus.

"I don't know," says Taylor. "I think I'll get the one with the red monster."

Once they leave the store, Gus has to get home.

"Um, thanks for today, you guys, I guess I'll be seeing you tomorrow," Gus says nervously.

"You'll be fine," says Fran. "You're the best skater there. Sleep well, yeah?"

"Don't worry. We'll meet you tomorrow," says Taylor.

Trucks
The trucks are the metal part that attaches to your deck and are usually made of aluminum.

Wheels
Small wheels are slower than big wheels. Hard wheels are used in street skating, while soft wheels are used for roads and rough surfaces.

The next morning, Gus wakes up with a dry mouth and a headache.

"I don't think I can go," he says to his mom.

"Honey, you've been looking forward to this for weeks. You have to go. I'll come with you if you want," she threatens, jokingly.

"No! I'll go by myself."

"I thought so," she laughs.

Gus walks slowly up to the skatepark. He's never seen this many people here! As he signs the registration form, he looks around for Daryl but can't see him. If he doesn't turn up, this will be a piece of cake! Gus heads to the half-pipe where the competition will be. Fran and Taylor run over to him.

"Hey Gus! How are you? Are you nervous?" shrieks Fran, jumping up and down.

"No. I'm cool. Have you seen Daryl?"

"Oh yeah. He's already up there." Fran points to the top of the half-pipe where Daryl stands with his board. Gus's heart sinks. The announcer starts yelling into the microphone. It's really hard to understand what he's saying, but it's clear that Daryl is about to skate.

Gus watches Daryl drop into the bowl with style.
He pumps well to get lots of height. Then he pulls
a grind at the top of the pipe. The entire crowd
claps and yells. He's doing really well. That makes
Gus feel worse.

The next person to step up to the top of the half-pipe is another skater that Gus doesn't know. The announcer introduces the new skater as Sam Hayes. Sam is obviously a good skater, but he's not as good as Daryl or Gus.

Then, finally, it's Gus's turn.

Gus slowly walks up to the top of the half-pipe, his heart beating in his head and his sweaty palms holding onto his board.

Without the grip tape on his deck, Gus is convinced that his board would slide into the half-pipe right now without him and everyone would laugh. Especially Daryl.

Gus looks up and can see Daryl smirking at him with his arms crossed over his chest. There is no way that he is going to beat me, thinks Gus.

All Gus has ever wanted to do is to skate.

This is his one chance to show everyone here that he is a skater and he should be on that team.

He takes a deep breath as he balances his board over the half-pipe.

The crowd are all silent.

Waiting for his next move.

Indoor skateparks
Some skateparks are built inside old warehouses.

Designer parks
This skatepark, called SMP Skatepark, opened in China in 2005 and covers over 144,000 square feet.

One more breath and he drops in. The crowd starts yelling and screaming as he gets more and more height.

Gus flies over the side of the half-pipe and grabs his board with one hand while holding onto the rim of the pipe with his other hand. Then he lands back in the half-pipe with ease and pumps for some more height.

It's time to nail that axle-stall for real. Gus is totally focussed. Nothing else in the world matters as much as this axle-stall right now. He gets height, he pulls it off. The crowd are yelling and screaming. He's done well and he knows it.

Gus looks up. Daryl is gone, but he can see his mom hiding in the back of the crowd, smiling at him.

Unusual shapes

Creating skateparks with different shapes means a whole new set of challenges for skaters.

Outdoor parks

Nothing beats skating outside on a sunny day!

Gus doesn't even notice the next few skaters. He's so pumped up he can't even listen properly to what Fran and Taylor are saying to him.

"Oh listen! Listen!" yells Fran. "They're about to announce the winner! I'm so nervous!"

"You're nervous?" asks Gus.

"Oh you know what I mean!" chides Fran.

Third place is given to someone they don't know.

"So you and Daryl must have got first and second," says Fran.

"And in second place, Sam Hayes!"

"What??" says Fran. "But that means...oh no."

Now Gus is really nervous. How could he or Daryl miss out on a place?

"It's been a very tough decision," says the announcer. "The standard here today has been very high. First place this year belongs to joint winners Daryl and Gus! Come and get your trophies!"

Gus and Daryl walk up on the podium. The announcer gives them their trophies. They try to glare at each other, but the crowd is yelling their names, clapping and whistling. They just can't keep scowling. Gus smiles at Daryl. Daryl smiles back. Finally, they laugh, shake hands and hold their trophies up to the crowd.

Glossary

Backside
When a trick or turn is executed with the skater's back facing the ramp or the obstacle.

Bail
To clear your board safely when a move goes wrong.

Deck
The wooden area of your skatebaord that you stand on.

Dropping in
A way of entering a bowl or half-pipe from the top.

Fakie
Riding your skateboard backward.

Frontside
When a trick or turn is performed with the skater's front facing the ramp or the obstacle.

Goofy stance
Skating with your right foot forward.

Grab
Using your hand or hands to hold the board during a move.

Grind
A move which involves scraping your skateboard's trucks along an object.

Grip tape
Sandpaperlike material stuck on the top of a deck to give riders more grip.

Kickturn
To turn your board by shifting the weight to the tail of the board and twisting.

Nollie
Short for a nose ollie.

Ollie
A move which sees you use your feet to pull the skateboard up into the air.

Pumping
Moving your bodyweight on your skateboard to build speed in a half-pipe.

Regular stance
When you skate with your left foot forward. Opposite of goofy stance.

Slide
A move where the underside of your deck slides along an object.

Street skating
Using street furniture, such as curbs, benches, and steps to perform tricks.

Switch stance
Riding your board and performing moves not using your normal stance.

Tail
The back end of a skateboard.

Tic-tac
A series of short kickturns performed in a row. It can give a boarder the momentum needed to travel across a flat area.

Trucks
The metal attachments bolted to the deck which connect the axles and wheels to the deck.

Vert ramp
A specially designed ramp for skateboarding with a horizontal area at its top.

Vert skating
Performing moves and tricks in a half-pipe or ramp. It usually involves getting air above the rim of the ramp or pipe.

Index